A GIFT FOR:

....

FROM:

....

Art Director: Chris Opheim
Editor: Theresa Trinder
Designer: Laura Elsenraat
Production Designer: Dan Horton

Published by Hallmark Gift Books,
A division of Hallmark Cards, Inc.,
Kansas City, MO 64141
Visit us on the Web at Hallmark.com.

ISBN: 978-1-59530-783-5
1BOK2224
Made in China
FEB16

NOW YOU'RE
40!

MILESTONES & MEMORIES FOR YOUR GENERATION

By Brandon M. Crose

> "Life really does begin at 40. Up until then you are just doing research."
>
> —Carl Jung

You've been called Generation X, the MTV Generation, even the "Forgotten" or "Ignored" Generation. Whatever. You were born in the so-called Me Decade, a time of self-exploration and no love for politicians. Your childhood heroes were Harrison Ford and Madonna, your spokesman was Kurt Cobain, and your fashion choices were...interesting. You lived the lifestyle of the music you loved. So no one understood you? Maybe they should have looked a little closer...

WHEN YOU WERE BORN...

IN THE NEWS

The Vietnam War came to a dramatic conclusion as over 1,000 American civilians and nearly 7,000 South Vietnamese refugees were evacuated from the roof of the U.S. Embassy in Saigon over the course of 18 hours. Communist forces took the city shortly after and later renamed it Ho Chi Minh City.

Reverend Jim Jones and over 900 of his followers—many of them small children—were found dead in and around the People's Temple in Jonestown, Guyana after drinking cyanide-laced Fla-Vor-Aid.

Your parents and many others watched, helpless, as Iran militants seized sixty-six American citizens and held most of them hostage at a U.S. embassy in Tehran for over a year.

WHEN YOU
WERE BORN

JIMMY CARTER BEGAN HIS
UNORTHODOX PRESIDENCY BY WALKING
THE INAUGURAL PARADE ROUTE
(INSTEAD OF RIDING IT IN AN ARMORED CAR).
ONE DAY LATER, HE EXTENDED AN
UNCONDITIONAL PRESIDENTIAL PARDON
TO ALL VIETNAM DRAFT DODGERS.

EVENTS

Neil Armstrong walked on the moon years before you were born, but space exploration was only just beginning: Viking 1 and Viking 2 searched for life on Mars, and the Skylab Space Station orbited the Earth for six years (before crashing into an Australian desert).

The fledgling Apple company began to sell their revolutionary Apple II personal computers, based on a design that Steve Jobs and Steve Wozniak developed in their California garage.

No advancement was so surprising as the announcement of another birth—the world's first baby conceived in vitro. The "test-tube baby" was born to Lesley and John Brown, an otherwise average British couple who quickly found themselves the center of a media maelstrom.

As science began to warn about the harmful nature of many drugs and artificial chemicals, many started reading the list of ingredients before adding an item to the grocery cart. Sales of health food rocketed to $1.6 billion by 1979!

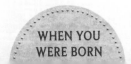

WHEN YOU
WERE BORN

MUSIC

You may not remember now, but "My Eyes Adored You" by Frankie Valli, "Silly Love Songs" by Paul McCartney, and "Angel in Your Arms" by Hot were likely among the first songs you ever heard.

Heavy metal bands Led Zeppelin, AC/DC, Aerosmith, and Van Halen blew out their amps; punk rockers The Sex Pistols, Patti Smith, The Velvet Underground, and The Ramones spoke to more rebellious-minded fans; and innovative rockers The Eagles and Fleetwood Mac changed the musical landscape.

Your parents lost a childhood icon with the untimely death of Elvis Presley. His final tour was quite a spectacle: that white caped suit, his martial arts moves, those sweaty scarves and the manic fans who reached for them… Elvis died at the age of 42, and upon hearing the news, heartbroken fans purchased millions more of his records.

**Were your parents into Disco?
Though the craze began with the Hues
Corporation's hit "Rock the Boat," no one
better embodied disco than the Bee Gees
with their hits "Stayin' Alive," "Night Fever,"
and "How Deep Is Your Love."**

WHEN YOU
WERE BORN

MOVIES

Your parents may have been one of the first to hear John Williams' fanfare and see those huge yellow titles disappearing into space. Few expected *Star Wars* to become the phenomenon it did, selling a record $256 million in tickets and an unheard-of $2.6 billion in toys, posters, books, lunchboxes, and other merchandise.

Other science fiction classics that came out around this time included blockbusters like *Superman*, *Close Encounters of the Third Kind*, *Alien*, and *Star Trek: The Motion Picture*.

Television just wasn't big enough for Jim Henson's Muppets. *The Muppet Movie* memorably featured Kermit the Frog performing "Rainbow Connection," which became a hit song—and was even nominated for an Oscar!

Other big movies your parents might have seen in the theater: *Jaws, Rocky, Grease, Taxi Driver, Annie Hall, Apocalypse Now* and, let us not forget, *Animal House* (a movie that inspired many a toga party).

WHEN YOU
WERE BORN

NOW SHOWING:

STAR WARS

THE MUPPET MOVIE

ROCKY

TV

Your parents' favorite shows may have included *All in the Family, Laverne and Shirley, Happy Days, Three's Company, Charlie's Angels,* or *The Waltons.*

A show about a single professional woman was daring for its time, but *The Mary Tyler Moore Show* won the Emmy Award for Outstanding Comedy Series three years in a row and later launched three spin-off series!

Saturday Night Live was born around the same time you were, launching the careers of Bill Murray, Chevy Chase, Dan Akroyd, Steve Martin, and many, many others.

If your parents watched anything other than *Roots* between January 23 and 30, 1977, then they were in the minority. An incredible 85% of the viewing public watched the twelve-hour miniseries adaptation of Alex Haley's novel.

WHEN YOU
WERE BORN

Gymnast Nadia Comăneci of Romania became the first athlete to score a perfect 10.0 at the Olympic games. Not bad for a 14-year old!

Former Olympic champion Leon Spinks challenged Muhammad Ali for the World Heavyweight Title and won it in a split decision. Ali, however, regained the title seven months later.

There's a reason he was the world's top-earning tennis player by the end of the decade—Bjorn Borg won a record five consecutive Wimbledon Singles Championships between 1976 and 1980.

Reggie Jackson hit three home runs in the final game of the World Series, helping secure victory for the New York Yankees over the Los Angeles Dodgers.

WHEN YOU
WERE BORN

POP CULTURE

The most popular baby boy names of the time were Michael, Jason, Christopher, David, and James. Jennifer, Melissa, Amy, Heather, and Jessica were most popular for baby girls.

The short-lived Disco Era brought flashing lights, spinning mirror balls, and polyester clothes. Perhaps your father still has his favorite leisure suit in a closet somewhere?

More married mothers were joining the workplace, but women with 4-year college degrees still made less than men with no more than an 8th grade education.

Minimum wage was between $2.10 and $2.90, and the median household income was approximately $11,000. A single-family home may have cost your parents around $57,200. (Or they could have purchased the former home of Al Capone in Pine Hill, New Jersey, on the market at this time, for $180,000.)

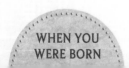

WHEN YOU
WERE BORN

WHEN YOU WERE A KID...

Ronald Reagan won the presidential election over incumbent Jimmy Carter in a historic landslide. The "Reagan Revolution" promised to restore "the great, confident roar of American progress and growth and optimism."

But did you know that Reagan had been president before...of the Screen Actors Guild, that is? You're too young to have seen many of his films, like *King's Row* and *Bedtime for Bonzo,* but your grandparents could probably give you some spoilers.

> You probably remember exactly where you were when you learned about the Challenger tragedy. Millions watched in horror as the space shuttle—whose crew included Christa McAuliffe, a school teacher—exploded moments after takeoff.

No one likes Mondays, but October 19th, 1987 was particularly bad: after several months of record gains, the Dow Jones plummeted 508 points—nearly 23% of its total value.

WHEN YOU WERE A KID

EVENTS

Most thought the AIDS epidemic was only a threat to some…until 13-year-old Ryan White acquired the virus through a blood transfusion and fought courageously to educate the world that this deadly disease was a threat to all.

The wreck of the RMS Titanic was at last found—broken in two and 12,000 feet under the North Atlantic. What you didn't know was that this discovery happened during a top-secret Navy mission to find the remains of two Cold War-era nuclear submarines.

Did your family purchase a new Cometron or Comet Catcher telescope to watch the once-in-a-lifetime passing of Halley's Comet in 1986? This orbiting ball of ice and dust passes Earth approximately once every 76 years.

Slain civil rights leader Martin Luther King, Jr. was honored with the dedication of a new national holiday, though initially, only 27 states observed it.

WHEN YOU
WERE A KID

MUSIC

Some of your favorite songs might have included "Girls Just Want to Have Fun" by Cyndi Lauper, "(You Gotta) Fight For Your Right (To Party)" by The Beastie Boys, or maybe you were one of the millions "Hangin' Tough" with boy band phenomenon New Kids on the Block, one of the world's best-selling groups of all time.

First featured in a commercial for the California Raisin Industry, four singing raisins spawned four albums, two TV specials, and a host of merchandise. The shriveled superstars are now part of the Smithsonian's permanent collection.

You didn't just listen to your music—
you watched it, too! VH1 joined MTV
to bring you trendsetting music videos by
80s icons like Madonna, Michael Jackson,
Cyndi Lauper, and Peter Gabriel.

Maybe you also watched the broadcast of Live Aid (along with 1.9 billion all over the world). A benefit to relieve famine in Ethiopia, the American concert closed with USA for Africa's hit "We Are the World."

MOVIES

Blockbuster popcorn flicks reigned supreme: you probably saw *Indiana Jones and the Temple of Doom, Ghostbusters,* and *Back to the Future* in the theater. Several times.

Whether you saw his movies when they came out or years later (once you were "old enough"), John Hughes may have been your personal Shakespeare. Many of his films, including *Sixteen Candles, The Breakfast Club, Pretty in Pink,* and *Ferris Bueller's Day Off,* remain classics today.

Other favorites may have included *The Princess Bride, The Goonies, The Muppets Take Manhattan,* and one that was almost certain to give you nightmares: *Gremlins.*

"Movie night" didn't always mean going to the theater— all you had to do was rent a VHS tape from the local video store and pop it into your VCR. (Let's just hope you didn't forget to rewind!)

WHEN YOU
WERE A KID

TV

Your favorite shows may have included Saturday morning cartoons *He-Man and the Masters of the Universe, She-Ra: Princess of Power, G.I. Joe, Rainbow Brite, Thundercats, The Care Bears Family, Inspector Gadget, Adventures of the Gummi Bears*, and *The Transformers.*

Speaking of Saturday morning, what better time to sit down with a big bowl of Cap'n Crunch or Fruity Pebbles and join your little blue friends for a Smurfing good adventure? *The Smurfs* was originally the brainchild of Belgian comic artist Peyo.

Not all your favorite shows were cartoons: you may have taken after *Punky Brewster's* unique fashion sense, *Fraggle Rock* might have been your idea of an ideal home, and you probably still remember the theme song to *Reading Rainbow.*

Or perhaps you sat down on Friday nights for T.G.I.F., a lineup of family-friendly shows, including *Full House, Family Matters*, and *Perfect Strangers.* ABC's plan was to entice folks to watch a "block" of programming, as opposed to just one show. (As you may remember, it worked.)

WHEN YOU WERE A KID

The American stars of the 1984 Olympic Games in Los Angeles were track-and-field athlete Carl Lewis, who took four gold medals, and gymnast Mary Lou Retton, whose gold medal performance in the individual all-around competition won her the adoration of many young aspiring athletes.

Before his illegal betting got him ousted from baseball, Cincinnati Reds batter Pete Rose surpassed 4,191 hits to break a record set 57 years earlier by Ty Cobb.

By 1987, 49.5% of American homes had cable TV. And the most popular cable channel by far? ESPN, with 60 million subscribers by the end of the decade.

Because of the success of sports television, you began to hear more about lesser-known sports, such as volleyball, water polo, wrestling, monster truck shows, and car racing.

WHEN YOU
WERE A KID

POP CULTURE

It was a great time to be a kid: you could beg your parents for Cabbage Patch Dolls (or Garbage Pail Kids if you were more subversive minded), slap bracelets, Pogo Balls, jelly shoes, and action figures from pretty much any cartoon you watched: *He-Man, My Little Pony, G.I. Joe, Transformers...*

The Nintendo Entertainment System may have been your first home gaming console. "Mario" and "Zelda" became household names as the gray and black box sold over 60 million units in its first two years.

An instant classic joined the "funnies" section of your newspaper: Bill Watterson's "Calvin and Hobbes," which taught you that tigers will do anything for a tuna fish sandwich.

Remember Rainforest Crunch? As Ben & Jerry's Ice Cream began distributing its trademark pints outside of New England, the entire nation went crazy for their favorite flavors.

WHEN YOU WERE A KID

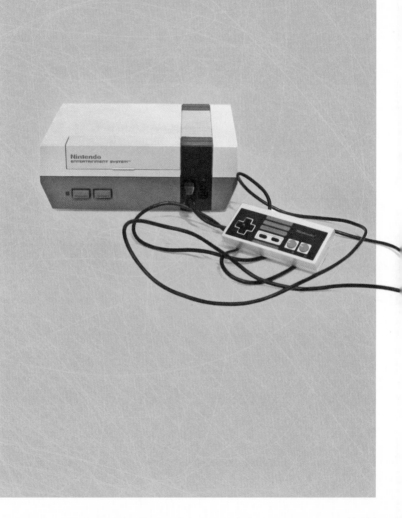

WHEN YOU WERE A TEENAGER...

IN THE NEWS

The World Trade Center bombing of 1993, while not the disaster its terrorist organizers had hoped, still resulted in the injury of over a thousand people and the deaths of six.

All fifty-one days televised, the standoff between followers of David Koresh and federal agents at a Waco, Texas compound ended with the deaths of over eighty people.

Still reeling from race riots after the Rodney King trial just two years earlier, Los Angeles was rocked by an early morning earthquake measuring 6.6 on the Richter Scale. It lasted only 40 seconds, but that was long enough to destroy several buildings and freeways, killing 55 people.

WHEN YOU
WERE A TEEN

George H. W. Bush was elected 41st President of the United States, defeating Michael Dukakis with only 50.1% of eligible voters casting a ballot.

"Today the majority of South Africans, black and white, recognize that apartheid has no future." After 27 years in prison for resisting a government that valued white lives over black, Nelson Mandela was free to continue his efforts to abolish apartheid.

Your world maps at school were now out of date: the Soviet Union dissolved, marking an official end to the Cold War.

Genetic modification allowed farmers to begin growing produce that was larger and more resistant to insecticides, though some scientists worried about the effects that these altered crops could have on the environment.

Continuous research in drugs suppressing the Human Immunodeficiency Virus (HIV), once considered a death sentence, led to more effective treatments—and longer lives.

WHEN YOU WERE A TEEN

MUSIC

If you were lucky enough to attend Lollapalooza in its first several years, you may have seen alternative rockers Jane's Addiction, Nine Inch Nails, Violent Femmes, Tool, The Smashing Pumpkins, or Rage Against the Machine live in concert.

A debut album by Dr. Dre, *The Chronic,* went platinum three times, bringing "Gangsta Rap" into the public eye and also launching the career of Snoop Dogg.

Other hit songs often heard on your Sony Discman might have included Sir Mix-a-Lot's "Baby Got Back," Boyz II Men's "I'll Make Love to You," and Green Day's "Longview."

WHEN YOU
WERE A TEEN

Musical icon of your teenage years, Kurt Cobain died at the home he shared with his wife, Courtney Love, of an apparent self-inflicted gunshot wound. He was just 27.

NOW SHOWING:

JURASSIC PARK

ACE VENTURA: PET DETECTIVE

PULP FICTION

MOVIES

Popcorn blockbusters were still king,
and new computer technology allowed
for special effects on a previously
unimagined scale. *Jurassic Park* paved
the way for future CGI spectacles.

Denzel Washington starred in two landmark films—
as the slain civil rights leader in *Malcolm X* and a lawyer
who fights to protect the rights of an HIV-positive
man in *Philadelphia*.

Forrest Gump introduced the philosophy "Life is like
a box of chocolates," and Jim Carrey became the
funny man of the decade with hit movies *Ace Ventura:
Pet Detective* and *Dumb and Dumber.*

Other memorable hit movies of your teenage years
include *Schindler's List, Pulp Fiction, Legends of the Fall,
Wayne's World, Léon: The Professional, Groundhog Day,*
and *The Shawshank Redemption.*

WHEN YOU
WERE A TEEN

TV

MTV's *Rock the Vote* series might have sparked an interest in politics. While President George H.W. Bush declined to appear at a televised "town hall" composed of MTV viewers, Bill Clinton did. Young voter turnout increased by more than 20% for the 1992 election... and guess who won?

Millions watched minute-by-minute televised coverage of scandals—from the O.J. Simpson police chase and trial to the Tonya Harding/Nancy Kerrigan assault.

A former politician and successful news anchor, Jerry Springer is better known as the host of the shockingly disturbing (and wildly popular) *Jerry Springer Show.*

Other memorable shows that you probably enjoyed in your teenage years include *My So-Called Life*, *Kids in the Hall*, *Friends* and, of course, *The Simpsons.*

WHEN YOU WERE A TEEN

The "Dream Team"—the first U.S. Olympic team to include NBA stars—achieved Olympic greatness in Barcelona. "It was like Elvis and the Beatles put together…like traveling with 12 rock stars," claimed their coach, Chuck Daly.

Basketball was big news, but baseball fans were not pleased when a 257-day strike led to the cancellation of the 1994 World Series.

Twenty years after losing the World Heavyweight Title to Muhammad Ali (and after ten years away from heavyweight competitions), George Foreman reclaimed his title by knocking out Michael Moorer in ten rounds.

After stumbling in two previous Olympic competitions, American speed skater Dan Jensen exemplified perseverance by taking home the gold medal *and* setting a new world record in the 1994 Winter Olympics' 1,000-meter event.

WHEN YOU
WERE A TEEN

"You've got mail!" You were probably checking e-mail, joining chat rooms, and browsing the Web on full-service programs like America Online, Prodigy, and CompuServe. If you were lucky, your parents may have even installed an extra phone line to "log on" without getting "booted" when the telephone rang.

Plaid and flannel shirts and worn-out jeans were the height of grunge fashion, you were pretty cool if you had a pager, the much-disliked New Coke was replaced with Coca-Cola Classic, and highly collectible Beanie Babies were *definitely* going to be worth a lot of money someday.

The Sega Genesis and Super Nintendo picked up where your trusty Nintendo left off, featuring cutting-edge 16-bit graphics and starting the race between the two video game giants.

Los del Río couldn't have known what monster they had created with "Macarena," which almost certainly became a synchronized fixture of your school dances and wedding parties. Like the hokey pokey or the electric slide before it, you probably still remember how the Macarena is done.

WHEN YOU
WERE A TEEN

WHEN YOU WERE IN YOUR 20s...

IN THE NEWS

September 11th, 2001. We will never forget.

In response to the attacks of 9/11, the Department of Homeland Security was formally established to "detect, prepare for, prevent, protect against, respond to, and recover from terrorist attacks within the United States."

United States and allies invaded Iraq on suspicion of its government having weapons of mass destruction. Though Saddam Hussein was removed from power, the Iraq War would officially continue for the next nine years, resulting in countless civilian casualties.

You'd witnessed the Challenger explosion, and you watched again as the space shuttle Columbia unexpectedly disintegrated after its return from a successful 16-day mission. All seven astronauts were killed, and debris from the shuttle rained across hundreds of miles of Texas countryside.

No one expected the devastation of Hurricane Katrina. The Category Four storm claimed the lives of nearly 2,000 New Orleans natives...and the homes of many, many more.

IN YOUR 20s

EVENTS

Computers had changed quite a lot since monochrome monitors and floppy discs, but one thing remained the same: their internal clocks had never been programmed to recognize the year 2000. Fearing a technological apocalypse, computer programmers raced to fix the Y2K Bug.

The Human Genome Project—a massive undertaking by scientists from the United States, United Kingdom, Germany, France, Japan, and China—announced that it had finally mapped all known human genes.

Massachusetts became the first state in the union to issue marriage licenses to same-sex couples.

A massive earthquake measuring 9.0 on the Richter Scale loosed a disastrous tsunami on Southeast Asia, killing over 225,000 and displacing 1.2 million more.

IN YOUR 20s

Y2K

MUSIC

You once listened to your music on cassette tapes, then CDs...and then it became digital! You may have first heard about MP3s via the file-sharing program Napster, which was sued for copyright infringement. No worries, though—just three years later you were able to make perfectly legal transactions at the iTunes Store.

American Idol launched the careers of talented performers Kelly Clarkson, Carrie Underwood, Chris Daughtry, and Jennifer Hudson. (As well as musical oddity William Hung.)

There were always girl bands, but never quite like this. TLC, Destiny's Child, and the Spice Girls were breaking ground—and breaking records—as *Scary, Baby, Ginger, Posh,* and *Sporty* became the most widely recognized household names since *John, Paul, George,* and *Ringo*.

Other hit songs from this time include "Breathe" by Faith Hill, "Hanging by a Moment" by Lifehouse, and "Hot in Herre" by Nelly.

IN YOUR 20s

NOW SHOWING:

LORD OF THE RINGS

GLADIATOR

A BEAUTIFUL MIND

George Lucas released the long-awaited prequel to the original *Star Wars* trilogy that was born when you were—*Episode I: The Phantom Menace.* Despite its mixed reviews, it was by far the top-grossing film of its year.

Swords and sorcery fans were validated at last by the sudden popularity of fantasy films: muggles worldwide rejoiced as the *Harry Potter* series began releasing one movie per year, and Peter Jackson's massively epic (and epically massive) *Lord of the Rings* film trilogy was the movie event of the decade.

Marvel superheroes started to find themselves in successful movies: *X-Men* and *Spider-Man* were both blockbusters, paving the way for many more successful superhero franchises...

Other familiar movies from this time might include *Monster's Ball, Amélie, The Sixth Sense, American Beauty, The Matrix, Gladiator, Almost Famous,* and *A Beautiful Mind.*

TV

Starring Kiefer Sutherland, each season of *24* depicted, in real time, a (very eventful) day in the life of counterterrorism specialist Jack Bauer. This novel approach to serial drama proved very popular with critics and fans.

Spanning nine seasons and four lead actors, *The X-Files* aired its final episode, but conspiracy fans wouldn't have to wait too long for their next mystery fix: *Lost* premiered two years later, featuring an incredible two-hour-long pilot that cost as much as fourteen million dollars to produce.

Other popular shows you watched may have included *Who Wants to Be a Millionaire?*, *ER*, *Friends*, *Frasier*, *Law & Order*, *Everybody Loves Raymond*, *C.S.I.: Crime Scene Investigation*, and *Will & Grace*.

IN YOUR 20s

Megapopular "reality TV" shows such as *Survivor, America's Next Top Model,* and *Dancing with the Stars* began to eclipse scripted dramas and comedies.

Though his legacy as "the greatest basketball player of all time" was already secure, Michael Jordan came out of retirement once more to play for the Washington Wizards. He promised to donate his salary to a relief fund for the victims of 9/11.

The 2002 Winter Olympics were held in Salt Lake City, with the men's United States snowboarding team sweeping the podium with all three medals, though Norway took home the most gold medals overall.

Michelle Kwan's clean programs and deep, quiet edges earned her numerous figure skating medals and championships, making her one of the most popular female athletes for over a decade.

Long-beleaguered Boston Red Sox fans had their day when their team beat the St. Louis Cardinals to win their first World Series Championship in eighty-six years. The "Curse of the Bambino" was at last reversed!

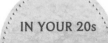
IN YOUR 20s

POP CULTURE

Crocs were in, low-carb diets like Atkins were all the rage, young people were abuzz with energy drinks and, after 9/11, it seemed that everyone had an American flag sticker on their car window or bumper.

From the television you watched to the songs on the radio, popular culture seemed obsessed with youth and the young. Teen pop sensations The Backstreet Boys, Britney Spears, 'N Sync, and Christina Aguilera were everywhere you looked, and the most popular TV shows included *The Simpsons, Friends,* and *South Park.*

Unlike your parents, who may have been married in their early 20s, you were more likely to wait until your mid- to late 20s before taking the plunge.

If you had children in your 20s, you were most likely to name them Jacob, Michael, Joshua, Matthew, or Ethan (if boys); Emily, Emma, Madison, Hannah, or Olivia (if girls).

IN YOUR 20s

WHEN YOU WERE IN YOUR 30s...

IN THE NEWS

From humble beginnings to 44th President of the United States, Barack Obama showed the world that the American dream is very much alive.

Haiti was hit by a magnitude-7 earthquake, devastating the small Caribbean country and displacing 1.5 million people from their homes.

An explosion on an oil rig fifty miles off the coast of Louisiana killed eleven workers and eventually resulted in the worst oil spill in U.S. history—an estimated 172 million gallons of crude oil permeated the Gulf coast... a disaster fifteen times greater than that of the Exxon Valdez.

Former Cold War enemies Russia and the United States signed the New Strategic Arms Reduction Treaty, promising that, by the year 2021, both countries would reduce their number of strategic nuclear missile launchers by half.

Following an international manhunt lasting almost ten years and two presidencies, U.S. military forces at last found Osama bin Laden, architect of the 9/11 attacks.

IN YOUR 30s

Your first "smartphone" may have been an Apple iPhone 3GS or a Motorola Droid. The hardware in either of these far exceeded the computing power that brought Neil Armstrong to the moon (and it even made phone calls!).

The "Great Recession," which began with the collapse of AIG, Lehman Brothers, and Bear Sterns, made it difficult for young people, perhaps you or your friends, to find a job or buy a house—and made the terms "subprime mortgage crisis" and "government bailout" hot topics of debate.

We learned that there's water on the moon! Or, *in* the moon—though its surface is as dry as any desert on Earth, frozen water beneath the moon's surface could someday be used to support human colonies. It's the stuff of science fiction! Or is it?

Almost 23 million Americans watched the royal wedding ceremony of Prince William and Kate Middleton, Duchess of Cambridge, at Westminster Abbey in London.

IN YOUR 30s

The world was stunned to learn that Michael Jackson died of a drug overdose less than a month before his sold-out concerts in London. Grieving fans bought 35 million of his albums, making Jackson the best-selling artist of 2009.

Green Day, a familiar band from your teenage years, turned their Grammy award-winning album *American Idiot* into a Broadway musical. The original cast recording *also* won a Grammy Award for Best Musical Show Album.

With the option to buy your music online by the song or album—and Amazon.com entering the MP3 business— digital downloads eclipsed sales of the physical CD.

Some hit songs you might have downloaded included "Love the Way You Lie" by Eminem (featuring Rihanna), "Moves like Jagger" by Maroon 5 (featuring Christina Aguilera), and "Call Me Maybe" by Carly Rae Jepsen.

IN YOUR 30s

MOVIES

Precious—a harrowing tale of abuse, poverty and, ultimately, hope—introduced the world to talented actress Gabourey Sidibe and earned a well-deserved Best Supporting Actress for Mo'Nique.

Kathryn Bigelow became the first woman to win Best Director at the Academy Awards for *The Hurt Locker,* which depicted the story of a bomb-disposal team during the Iraq War.

A French black-and-white silent film, *The Artist,* was nominated for ten Oscars and took home five, including Best Picture, Best Director, and Best Actor.

It wasn't all superhero movies—you may have also enjoyed *The Blind Side, Up, The Town, Midnight in Paris, The Fighter, The Help,* or *My Week with Marilyn.*

IN YOUR 30s

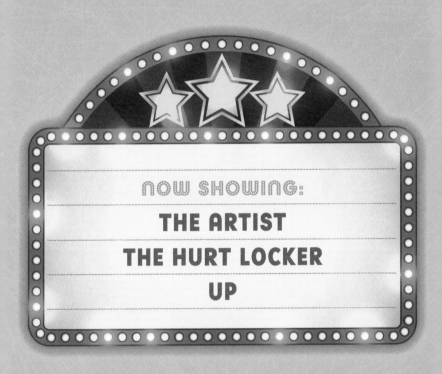

NOW SHOWING:

THE ARTIST

THE HURT LOCKER

UP

Music isn't the only thing that's gone digital—now you can watch TV shows on your computer, too!

In fact, more and more people (and maybe you were one of them) began canceling their expensive cable packages in favor of online streaming services such as Netflix, Hulu, and Amazon Prime.

Were you on Team CoCo? Unhappy with ratings, NBC took the *Tonight Show* away from brand-new host Conan O'Brien and returned the late-night television staple to former host Jay Leno. O'Brien's fans rallied behind him, resulting in a lot of embarrassing headlines for NBC.

Other shows you may have watched (or still do!) include *The Office, Modern Family, The Big Bang Theory, Castle, Glee, Community, The Good Wife, NCIS, Bones, Parenthood,* and *House.*

IN YOUR 30s

SPORTS

American cyclist Lance Armstrong survived cancer to take home seven Tour de France titles—only to have all of them stripped away after allegations of performance-enhancing drug use.

The United States broke the record again for the most medals won at a single Winter Olympics in 2010, with Americans Bode Miller and Shaun White having memorable breakout performances.

Tennis fans witnessed the longest match in tennis history as American John Isner played Nicolas Mahut of France at the Wimbledon Championships over the course of three days, for a total of 11 hours and 5 minutes.

Led by the "Big Three"—LeBron James, Chris Bosh, and Dwyane Wade—the Miami Heat won two NBA Finals against the Oklahoma City Thunder and then the San Antonio Spurs.

IN YOUR 30s

POP CULTURE

Technology is everywhere—chances are you have at least one of the following: a GPS in your car, Bluetooth transmitter in your ear, an activity tracker on your wrist, or a sleep monitor under your mattress.

You have almost certainly discovered the Internet phenomenon that is YouTube—endless hours of homemade hilarity, officially licensed music videos, and some other things you wish you could forget.

Pong came out just several years before you were born, and since then, video games have evolved by eye-popping degrees. "Next-generation" consoles PlayStation 4 and the Xbox One are capable of graphics you likely never imagined a video game could have when you were playing Jungle Hunt on your Atari 2600 or Super Mario Bros. on your Nintendo Entertainment System.

IN YOUR 30s

Computers "grew up" with you, and now they're an everyday part of life: from social networking staples such as Facebook and Twitter, all those blogs you follow (or perhaps write), interoffice chat applications and video conferencing, to even the news you read.

NOW YOU'RE 40!

And you're in good company! Look who else is in their 40s:

- Tiger Woods, golfer
- Idina Menzel, actress and singer
- Angelina Jolie, actress and humanitarian
- Brett Favre, football player
- Daniel Tosh, comedian
- will.i.am, musician
- Leonardo DiCaprio, actor
- Shaquille O'Neal, basketball player
- Wes Anderson, director
- Sofia Vergara, actress
- Zadie Smith, author
- Tina Fey, actress and writer
- Bradley Cooper, actor
- Jamie Oliver, chef
- Stefi Graf, tennis player

"The first forty years of life
give us the text; the next thirty
supply the commentary."

—*Arthur Schopenhauer*

"When I passed forty I dropped
pretense, 'cause men like women
who got some sense."

—*Maya Angelou*

"At twenty years of age,
the will reigns; at thirty the wit;
at forty the judgment."

—*Benjamin Franklin*

DID YOU ENJOY THIS BOOK?

We would love to hear from you.

Please send your comments to:
Hallmark Book Feedback
P.O. Box 419034
Mail Drop 100
Kansas City, MO 64141

Or e-mail us at:
booknotes@hallmark.com